Mr Steggels
Selective Achievement Tests
Level 3

Suitable for ages 9 – 11

Each test contains 35 mixed questions

- 15 general ability
- 10 reading comprehension
- 10 mathematics

A score summary chart is printed at the end of each test

Contents

Test 1	page 2
Test 2	page 12
Test 3	page 22
Test 4	page 32
Test 5	page 42

Solutions

Test 1	page 52
Test 2	page 53
Test 3	page 55
Test 4	page 57
Test 5	page 59

Copyright © 2017 Simon Steggels
All rights reserved

No part of this book may be reproduced, stored in a retrieval system, communicated or transmitted in any form or by any means without prior written permission. All inquiries should be made to the publisher.

ISBN 978-0-6480967-2-6

Published by
Advanced Instruction Pty Ltd
www.advancedinstruction.com.au

© MR STEGGELS ADVANCED INSTRUCTION PTY LTD

Test 1

Read the text and answer questions 1—5

Mathematics investigation—How far can I jump?
1. Find a grass area. The park is a great choice. You'll need a tape measure for this activity. 2. Mark a spot on the ground. Stand with your feet together and jump forward. Mark the spot where you landed. Now measure the distance you jumped in centimeters. 3. Draw a picture of what you did and write down how far you jumped. 4. Repeat what you did two more times and record those distances too.

Draw a picture of what you did:	How far I jumped: Jump 1: _____ cm Jump 2: _____ cm Jump 3: _____ cm

5. Now, use the Internet to research "long jump world record". Fill out these details.

   a) What is the world record for long jump? _____ m

   b) Who jumped this distance? _____

   c) What year did this happen? _____

In a long jump competition, a person gets to run before they jump. This time you are going to run.

6. Put a marker on the ground that you will notice, like a hat. Now take twenty big steps away from the marker, then turn and run. Jump when you get to the marker. Measure how far you jumped this time.
7. Repeat what you did two more times and record those distances too.

Draw a picture of what you did:	How far I jumped: Jump 1 _____ cm Jump 2 _____ cm Jump 3 _____ cm

8. Did you jump further this time? Explain why.

9. Why was it important to jump three times, and not just once?

10. Extension (optional). How much further than your best jump is the world record jump?

© MR STEGGELS ADVANCED INSTRUCTION PTY LTD

1. This text can best be described as

   A   a problem
   B   a puzzle
   C   an investigation
   D   an experiment

2. Section 5 requires

   A   a tape measure
   B   a computer or device with access to the world wide web
   C   that the student repeat the jump three times
   D   a world record breaking long jump

3. Which is true?

   A   The extension question must be done by all students
   B   Section 5 requires adult supervision
   C   Questions 8 and 9 require only brief answers
   D   It is expected that students will jump further each time they repeat the jump

4. The second series of jumps is different from the first because the student must

   A   jump three times
   B   draw a picture
   C   take a run up instead of jumping from a standing start
   D   compare it to the world record jump

5. Which word in the text has been used as both a noun and a verb?

   A   record
   B   jump
   C   further
   D   both A and B

© MR STEGGELS ADVANCED INSTRUCTION PTY LTD

6. Which letters are missing in this series?

    AB, FG, KL, ___, UV

    A   MN
    B   NO
    C   OP
    D   none of the above

7. One jug contains 1.9 L of milk. A second jug contains 2.5 L of milk. How much milk must be poured from the second jug into the first so that both jugs contain the same amount of milk?

    A   0.2 L
    B   0.3 L
    C   1.3 L
    D   4.4 L

8. In a certain code, the words **lips**, **slip** and **silt** are written 4873, 4785 and 8734, but not necessarily in that order. How would **list** be written using this code?

    A   8745
    B   8747
    C   4738
    D   8743

9. There were 70 students on the school bus. After 6 girls and 4 boys got off, there were half as many boys as girls on board. How many boys were on the bus to begin with?

    A   35
    B   30
    C   24
    D   22

10. A **desert** can best be described as

    A   fertile
    B   sweet
    C   arid
    D   cold

© MR STEGGELS ADVANCED INSTRUCTION PTY LTD

11. Which tile is missing in this series?

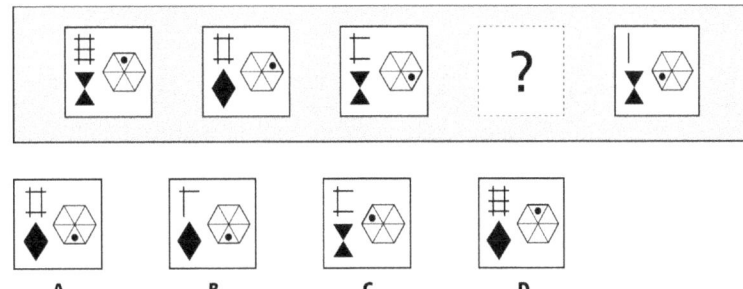

12. Which word has a different meaning from the other three?

    A   river
    B   estuary
    C   stream
    D   valley

13. Consecutive numbers follow each other in order, without gaps from smallest to largest. What is the smallest of three consecutive numbers that add up to 66?

    A   20
    B   21
    C   22
    D   63

14. One square weighs the same as two circles. One circle weighs the same as four triangles. How many squares weigh the same as eight triangles?

    A   1
    B   2
    C   4
    D   8

15. Which word can be placed before these words to make new, compound words?

    _____guard   _____boat   _____blood   _____line

    A   fishing
    B   red
    C   body
    D   life

© MR STEGGELS ADVANCED INSTRUCTION PTY LTD

Read the texts and answer questions 16—20

Text A

13/02/17

Att: Mr Scott
Principal
Grosvenor Public School

My son, Albert Edwards in class 3P, came home from school today sunburned on his nose, cheeks and ears. As you are no doubt aware, the temperature reached 37 degrees by lunchtime. How did he get sunburned when he should have been supervised in the shade?

Why was my son allowed to play outside in the sun without proper sun protection? Albert said that he played handball for over 40 minutes on the basketball court. Clearly your teaching staff is not policing the school's **no hat no play** rule. This is clearly unacceptable.

Children as young as Albert are not fully aware of the dangers of skin cancer. They need adults to look after their wellbeing. This did not happen. Now my son has a bad case of sunburn. I would like to know what you are going to do about it.

Sincerely,

Mrs Heather Edwards

Text B

Hey Patty,

How are you? Tried to call but couldn't get a hold of you. So, I thought I'd try to reach you on Messenger. You must be really busy settling into your new house.

Thanks heaps for the birthday present. I arrived home just in time to get it from the mailman outside my house. I love it! The scrapbook you made has so many great photos of us. Did you get them printed at a shop? The colours are amazing.

I really missed you at my party. All the girls from our class were there, and a couple of the boys, too. We played Marco Polo in the pool and had water bomb fights. Clara was a real pain in the neck (of course). I ignored her. Mum even hired a karaoke machine—it was so much fun listening to everyone singing so badly. She made our favourite dessert: banana cheesecake. Yum! Wish you could've been here.

Anyway, hope you're well. Give us a call soon if you can.

Love Amy xx

© MR STEGGELS ADVANCED INSTRUCTION PTY LTD

16. In text A, the letters **Att** stand for

    A   Attendance
    B   Attention
    C   Attachment
    D   Attack

17. The tone of Text B can best be described as **friendly** and **unofficial**. The tone of Text A can best be described as

    A   angry and unofficial
    B   relaxed and official
    C   angry and official
    D   unacceptable and unofficial

18. The main reason that Amy has written a message is

    A   to thank Patty for the birthday gift she gave her at her birthday party
    B   to see if Patty is enjoying her new school
    C   to invite Patty to her birthday party
    D   because she couldn't get Patty on the phone

19. We can conclude that Patty

    A   used to attend the same school as Amy
    B   did not attend Amy's birthday party
    C   has tasted Amy's mother's cheesecake before
    D   all of the above

20. What does Mrs Edwards find unacceptable?

    A   Her son, Albert, suffered sunburn on his nose, cheeks and ears
    B   Students were playing on such a hot day
    C   Teachers are not policing the **no hat no play** rule
    D   Mr Scott is not aware that students are playing outside without sun protection

21. Which can be worn on the head?

    A   souvlaki
    B   masseur
    C   bouquet
    D   beret

22. Find the rule connecting the numbers in the first row with those in the second row. Which number should replace the question mark?

1st row	4	7	11	16	22
2nd row	7	13	21	31	?

    A   41
    B   42
    C   43
    D   44

23. The Gongdatch is a strange bird. It moves by taking 2 steps forward and 1 step to the right. The river that it loves to drink from is 10 steps directly ahead. How many times will the Gongdatch step to the right before it reaches the river?

    A   4
    B   5
    C   9
    D   10

24. A **doctor** always works

    A   at a hospital
    B   during the day
    C   alone
    D   with patients

25. I tossed a coin three times. How many different results were possible?

    A   3
    B   6
    C   8
    D   9

26. **Merry** is to **glad** as **blunt** is to

   A sharp
   B unsharpened
   C acute
   D bright

27. What will this shape look like when it is flipped over the dotted line and rotated 90 degrees clockwise?

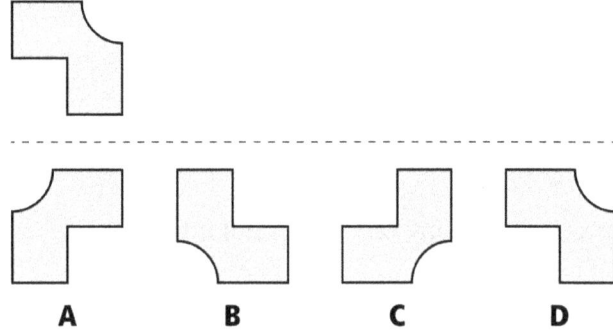

28. Rearrange these words into a coherent sentence

   and   the   day   feed   fly   during   butterflies

   If the first word of the new sentence is not **during**, the fourth word must be

   A day
   B fly
   C feed
   D butterflies

29. Which group of letters comes next in the series?

   wvx,   zya,   cbd,   _____

   A feg
   B edf
   C fge
   D dce

© MR STEGGELS ADVANCED INSTRUCTION PTY LTD

30. Which statement is true?

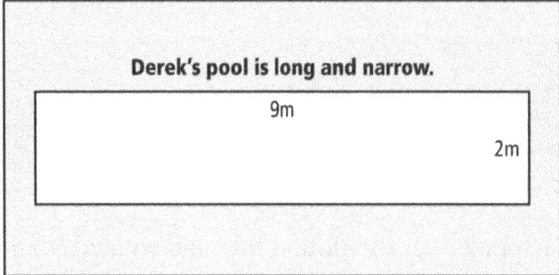
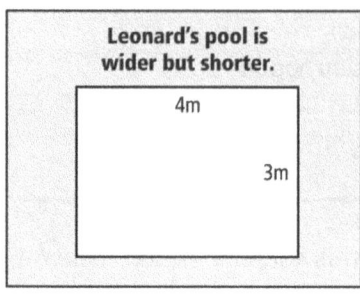

- A The area of Derek's pool is ¾ less than the area of Leonard's pool
- B Derek and Leonard's pools are equal in area
- C Derek's pool is 1½ times the area of Leonard's pool
- D Derek's pool is 1⅓ times the area of Leonard's pool

31. Unscramble these words to find the only one that is not a fruit

- A lmpu
- B egnaro
- C pnsiahc
- D oelnm

32. Which shape completes the larger pattern?

A 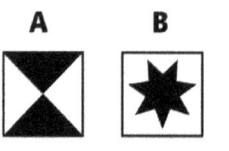 B  C 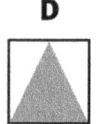 D

33. I made some cupcakes for $25 and sold them all for $65. If I made a profit of 40 cents on each cupcake, how many cupcakes did I sell?

- A 40
- B 16
- C 100
- D 160

34. Solve this visual puzzle

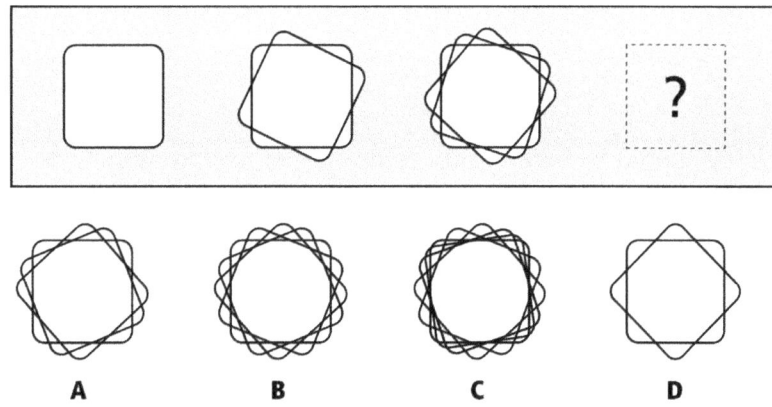

35. In a certain code, the word **revolt** is written as **ivelog**. In the same code, what is the word represented by the code **nrmfgv**?

   A   moment
   B   miners
   C   minute
   D   normal

© MR STEGGELS ADVANCED INSTRUCTION PTY LTD

END OF TEST

Test 2

Read the text and answer questions 1—5

'I really don't think we should be here,' said Frank. 'It's almost midnight.'

Greg pulled apart the chain metal fence. 'Come on. The place is totally deserted. Trust me. No one comes here anymore.' He gestured for Frank to climb through.

Frank hesitated. 'But everyone in our class says the place is haunted…'

'And that's why we're making this video!' said Greg. 'When they see we came here by ourselves, at night, we'll be the coolest kids in the school.'

Frank reluctantly climbed through the hole in the fence. 'I'm telling you this is a bad idea,' he said.

The pair walked across a large open forecourt. There were weeds growing through deep cracks in the concrete. A giant clown head loomed above them—the entrance to the Happy Mountain Amusement Park. The clown did not look happy. Its teeth had been smashed in with rocks and the sharp shards that were left looked like fangs. The eyes were black and there was a large hole in the forehead.

Suddenly, black shapes appeared in the sky. Frank shrieked.

'They're just bats,' said Greg dismissively.

Frank's eyes widened in terror. 'Bats?'

'They're everywhere around here. Come on! It's just up ahead.'

'But isn't that where the accident happened? With those kids…'

'Exactly!' Greg cried, and took off running, video camera at the ready. Frank shook his head in **frustration**. He had no choice but to follow.

Greg was too fast. Frank had to stop to catch his breath. He saw Greg climb over a wooden railing at the entrance to the Snappy Snake Coaster. He jumped down onto the tracks and ran into a tunnel just beyond the boarding platform.

'What are you doing?' Frank yelled. He was almost at the wooden railing when he heard rumbling. At first he thought it was thunder. Then he realised that it was coming from inside the tunnel.

The rumbling grew louder. The platform under Frank's feet began to shake violently. Then he heard wild laughter. It was the sound of children screaming their lungs out.

'Greg!' he called out. 'Do you hear that? Get out of there!'

Lights suddenly appeared in the tunnel. Frank watched in horror as the Snappy Snake Coaster train burst out of the tunnel and thundered through the loading area like an angry beast. Crazy laughter filled the air. The carriages were smashed and broken. There was no one on board…

© MR STEGGELS ADVANCED INSTRUCTION PTY LTD

1. Greg can best be described as _____ while Frank is _____.

   A   strong   weak
   B   reckless   cautious
   C   hesitant   terrified
   D   brave   cowardly

2. What word could best replace the word **frustration** as it is used in the text?

   A   defeat
   B   anger
   C   disappointment
   D   annoyance

3. Which is an example of a **simile**?

   A   Like an angry serpent
   B   A giant clown head loomed above them
   C   The Snappy Coaster train burst out of the tunnel
   D   The platform under Frank's feet began to shake violently

4. Which word means **emerged in a threatening way**?

   A   thundered
   B   appeared
   C   loomed
   D   burst

5. The author is suggesting that the Happy Mountain Amusement Park

   A   is still open to visitors
   B   caught fire and shut down
   C   is designed to be scary, not happy
   D   is, in fact, haunted

© MR STEGGELS ADVANCED INSTRUCTION PTY LTD

6. Choose the category to which the other words belong

    A   apple crumble
    B   cheesecake
    C   dessert
    D   trifle

7. **Mountain** is to **high** as _____ is to _____

    A   valley   low
    B   forest   wet
    C   desert   rain
    D   river   water

8. The saying **more or less** means

    A   more than or less than
    B   roughly, nearly, almost always
    C   equal to
    D   none of the above

9. I am more than 21 but less than 55. I am an odd number. There is a 4 in my number. How many different numbers could I be?

    A   4
    B   5
    C   7
    D   12

10. Ramsey is not as old as Clara. On his next birthday, Ollie will be as old as Ramsey is now. Bill is two years older than Clara. When listed from youngest to oldest, the children are

    A   Ollie, Clara, Ramsey, Bill
    B   Bill, Clara, Ollie, Ramsey
    C   Bill, Clara, Ramsey, Ollie
    D   Ollie, Ramsey, Clara, Bill

© MR STEGGELS ADVANCED INSTRUCTION PTY LTD

Use this calendar to answer questions 11—12

S	M	T	W	T	F	S
		1	2	3	4	5
6	7	8	9	10	11	12
13	14	15	16	17	18	19
20	21	22	23	24	25	26
27	28	29	30	31		

11. I attend swimming lessons on Thursdays whose dates are composite numbers and Saturdays whose dates are prime numbers. How many days did I attend swimming lessons this month?

    A   3
    B   4
    C   5
    D   6

12. There are seven months of the year that the calendar above could show. This is the sixth of these months in the year. Which month is shown on the calendar?

    A   December
    B   November
    C   July
    D   October

13. Rearrange all of the words to make a coherent sentence

    the   hat   student   was   there   without   that   teacher   a   saw   a

    The last word in the new sentence is

    A   teacher
    B   student
    C   hat
    D   without

14. If 4 rumberries and 1 digifuit weigh the same as 3 elmons, and 2 rumberries weigh the same as 1 digifruit, how many digifruit weigh the same as 1 elmon?

    A   1
    B   2
    C   3
    D   12

© MR STEGGELS ADVANCED INSTRUCTION PTY LTD

15. The word **opinion** has the same meaning as

    A   viewpoint
    B   outlook
    C   judgement
    D   all of the above

16. What number is missing from this number sentence?

    $$68 \times \underline{} = 238 \times 2$$

    A   4
    B   6
    C   7
    D   8

17. **Match** is to **fire** as **key** is to _____

    A   door
    B   car
    C   hole
    D   chain

18. I made this model of a staircase using blocks. How many more blocks will I need to make the staircase six steps high?

    A   12
    B   22
    C   42
    D   30

© MR STEGGELS ADVANCED INSTRUCTION PTY LTD

19. I walked from the Campsite to Blue Falls, then out to Rocky Point before returning to the Campsite. Blue Falls is on the way to Rocky Point, on the same path. What distance did I cover?

    A   23.4km
    B   33.4km
    C   45.8km
    D   66.8km

20. Which code matches the shape on the right?

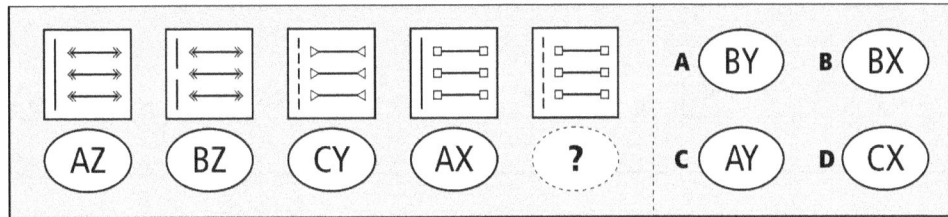

21. In a certain code, the word **plait** is written **kozrg**. How would the word **flushed** be written using the same code?

    A   uouhsvw
    B   uofhsvw
    C   uofshvw
    D   uofhswv

22. Which word can be used to end the first word and begin the second?

                      full_____ / _____pay

    A   back
    B   empty
    C   glass
    D   some

© MR STEGGELS ADVANCED INSTRUCTION PTY LTD

23. Which pattern comes next in the sequence?

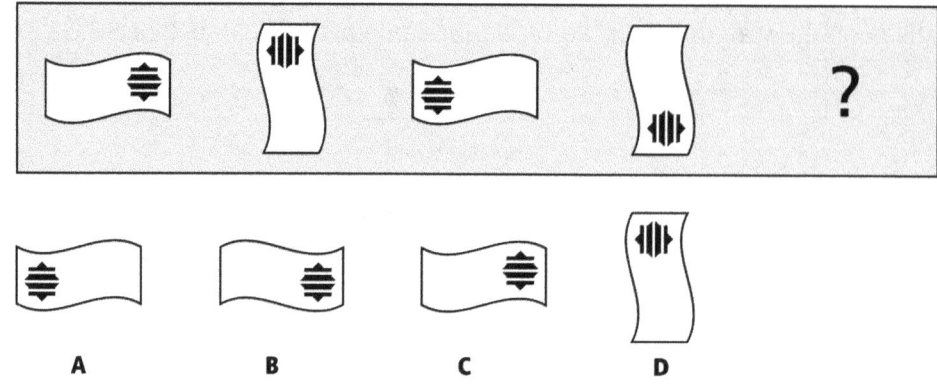

24. Which numbers need to be placed in the shapes to make the number sentences true?

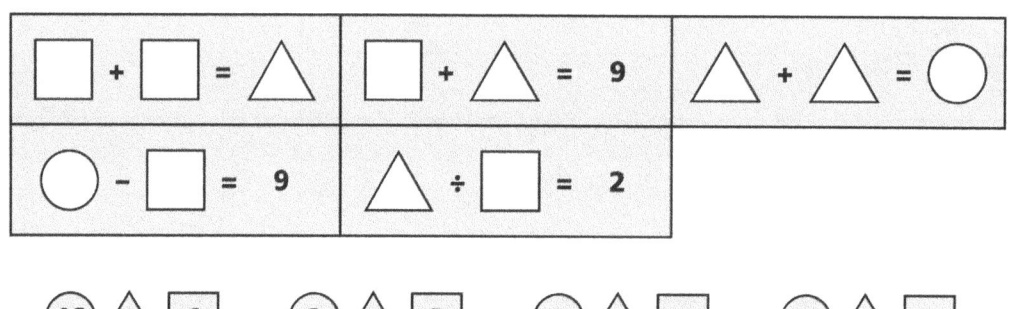

25. Which tile comes next in the pattern?

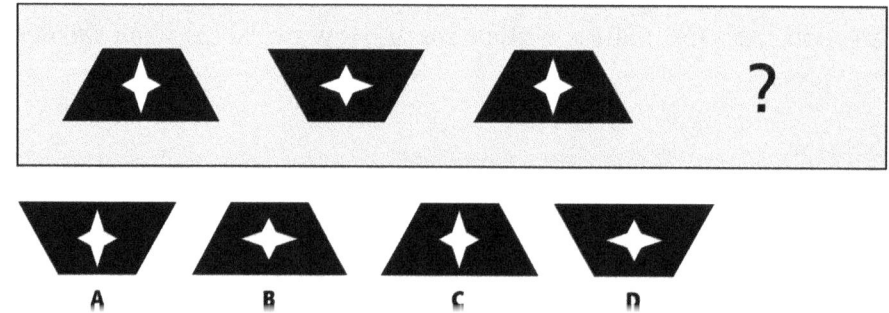

26. Which word means something that **burns very easily**?

   A   fire
   B   flammable
   C   burning
   D   explosion

27. Which word belongs in this group of similar words?

   London   Moscow   Tokyo   New Delhi

   A   New York
   B   Mexico
   C   Paris
   D   Egypt

28. Unscramble these jumbled letters and choose which one is **not a sport**

   A   lppo
   B   ciktrce
   C   lalbten
   D   utorc

29. If Tamara is older than Minny, and Susan is younger than Tamara, which statement must also be correct?

   A   Minny is the youngest of the three girls
   B   Susan is younger than Minny
   C   Susan and Minny are the same age
   D   Tamara is the eldest of the three girls

30. A **father** always has a

   A   wife
   B   child
   C   brother
   D   nephew

© MR STEGGELS ADVANCED INSTRUCTION PTY LTD

Read the text and answer questions 31—35

Hip Hip Hooray®
Party essentials

All your party needs in one place!

Free shipping on orders over $50 Australia wide!**

Check website for details

**Same day delivery is not available in all areas.

Shop by

ITEM
THEME
COLOUR
AGE
EVENT

Our warehouses are stocked with a huge range of party essentials, including toys, games, and hand-selected gifts.

We have every party decoration you can imagine—balloons, streamers, ribbons and banners. We also have a great range of cartoon table settings, including plates, cups and cutlery.

Haven't shopped with us before? Visit us today at

www.hiphiphooray.com

Take advantage our **cake decorating service!**

Choose from a huge range of delicious cakes in a variety of flavours and styles.

We even make individual cakes on request, featuring cartoon characters and superheroes.

All cakes made fresh daily!

Order online today!

DISCOUNT VOUCHER!

20% OFF

Coupon code G2SAVE

Enter coupon code at checkout before paying
Expiry date 01/12/2017

*minimum spend $100

© MR STEGGELS ADVANCED INSTRUCTION PTY LTD

31. The author of this text wants to

    A   persuade the reader to visit the Hip Hip Hooray® website and make a purchase
    B   provide information about the products and services offered by Hip Hip Hooray®
    C   attract new customers to buy from Hip Hip Hooray®
    D   all of the above

32. The author has made parts of the text stand out, by using

    A   exclamation marks
    B   italics
    C   bold text
    D   all of the above

33. We can conclude that same day delivery would not be available

    A   in major capital cities
    B   to people living in rural or country areas
    C   to customers who use the discount voucher
    D   because the postal service is not reliable

34. A customer wanting to buy products for a New Year's Eve party would most likely shop by

    A   item
    B   theme
    C   colour
    D   event

35. Which word means **no longer valid after a certain date**?

    A   coupon
    B   discount
    C   expiry
    D   voucher

END OF TEST

Test 3

1. What is the perimeter of this figure?

   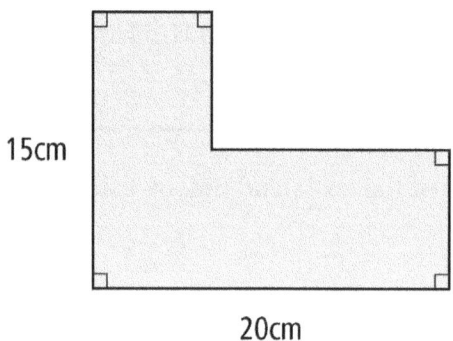

   A   35 cm
   B   55 cm
   C   70 cm
   D   impossible to calculate

2. **Broken** is to **repaired** as _____ is to _____

   A   strange   weird
   B   mean   kind
   C   male   man
   D   car   tyre

3. Which item of clothing is meant to be **knotted**?

   A   jacket
   B   brooch
   C   tie
   D   beret

4. In a certain code, **foal** is written ? + ^ / and **cruise** is written @ # $ % & >
   How would the word **careful** be written in the same code?

   A   @ ^ # > ? & /
   B   ? # & > @ $ +
   C   @ ^ # % & $ /
   D   @ ^ # > ? $ /

© MR STEGGELS ADVANCED INSTRUCTION PTY LTD

5. I went to the shop with a $5 note and a $2 coin. I spent $1.75 on a pen and $2.85 on a pad. How much change should I expect?

    A $3.60
    B $2.60
    C $2.40
    D $3.40

6. The word most opposite to **famous** is

    A   celebrity
    B   traitor
    C   unknown
    D   unfamous

7. How long was I at work if I started at 6.40am and finished at 3.15pm?

    A   9 hours and 55 minutes
    B   9 hours and 35 minutes
    C   8 hours and 55 minutes
    D   8 hours and 35 minutes

8. Which statement best describes this number sentence?

    $$250 - 75 - 75 - 75 = 25$$

    A   250 shared between 75 people gives 25 each
    B   250 shared between 3 people gives 25 each and 75 left over
    C   250 shared between 3 people gives 75 each
    D   250 shared between 3 people gives 75 each and 25 left over

9. Which is the odd word out?

    A   error
    B   blunder
    C   lie
    D   slip-up

Choose the best words to complete the passage

Long, long ago, in a faraway land, there lived a very handsome but _____ (10) prince. The King and Queen had spoiled him from a young age, giving him everything he desired. He had the very best of what money could buy. And he was always greedy for more. He wore the finest clothes, ate the finest food, and had the richest friends. But he still felt empty. None of his possessions could fill the emptiness. He wanted something that could not be _____ (11).

One day, while riding in the forest on his finest horse, the prince caught sight of a young lady gathering flowers at the side of the road. She bowed in respect then looked up at him. She was so beautiful that she almost took the Prince's breath away.

'What is your name?' he asked her.

'Annabelle, my Lord,' she replied humbly.

'Where do you live?' asked the Prince.

She _____ (12) further down the road. 'In a cottage just beyond the brook.'

The prince got down from his horse and went over to her. 'Who are the flowers for?'

'These are for my father. It is his birthday today,' she replied.

The prince was surprised that the young lady thought that wild flowers made a suitable gift. 'He will need more than flowers,' he said. 'I will buy him something. Or I will give him something of my own. What would he like? Name it and it shall be yours. A horse? A banquet? Gold!'

Annabelle smiled humbly. 'Thank you, but my father has no need for such things.'

The prince could not believe his ears. 'No need? Why, of course he does! What man on Earth does not want the finest of _____ (13) !'

'The things of this world do not last,' she replied. 'There is only one thing that lives on. Good day, Prince.' She bowed to him.

The prince watched as Annabelle walked into a small _____ (14) marked with gravestones. She stood in front of one for a moment, then bent down and placed the flowers at its base. 'Happy birthday, Father,' she said.

Something stirred deep within the Prince's soul. And he knew what it was that his heart desired most of all.

© MR STEGGLES ADVANCED INSTRUCTION PTY LTD

10. Choose the most suitable word for position 10

    A   evil
    B   lonely
    C   selfish
    D   kind

11. Choose the most suitable word(s) for position 11

    A   enjoyed for long
    B   bought or sold
    C   touched or held
    D   understood

12. Choose the most suitable word for position 12

    A   wandered
    B   shouted
    C   turned
    D   gestured

13. Choose the most suitable word(s) for position 13

    A   my possessions
    B   everything
    C   birthdays
    D   daughters

14. Choose the most suitable word for position 14

    A   clearing
    B   cottage
    C   church
    D   brook

© MR STEGGELS ADVANCED INSTRUCTION PTY LTD

15. The word **permanent** is most nearly opposite in meaning to

    A   solid
    B   fleeting
    C   marker
    D   ancient

16. I purchased these items. If I got all of the items for half price, the amount I paid was closest to

| book $12.95 | highlighter $3.56 | sticky tape $2.48 | ruler $0.96 | calculator $32.87 |

    A $52
    B $53
    C $27
    D $26

17. Which number completes the pattern?

X	2	3	7	11	12
Y	13	18	38	58	?

    A   60
    B   63
    C   68
    D   73

18. Which is the odd one out?

19. Choose two words, one from each group, to make a new word.

Group A	face	hair	hand	paint
Group B	some	shave	where	fair

The new word beings with

A   s
B   f
C   h
D   p

20. In a certain code, **pears** is written ! @ # $ % and **ticket** is written ^ & * ? @ ^

How would the word **carpets** be written in the same code?

A   & # $ ^ @ * %
B   * # $! @ ^ %
C   * # $! @ & %
D   none of the above

21. Which letter will end the first word and start the second word?

myt __ / __ ave

A   s
B   g
C   h
D   c

22. The value shown by the arrow is

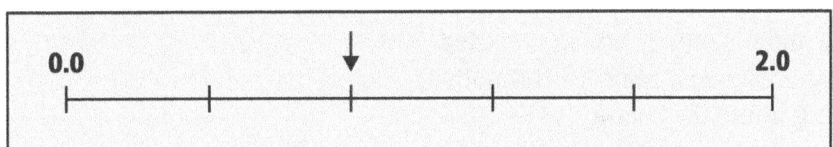

A   1.0
B   1.2
C   0.6
D   0.8

23. The numbers in each of the four patterns follow the same rule. What is the missing number?

| 8 | 23 | 13 | | 5 | 14 | 7 | | 6 | 17 | 9 | | 7 | 13 | ? |

   A   4
   B   5
   C   6
   D   7

24. In a certain code, the word **nature** is written **qdwxuh**. In the same code, how would the word **spoiled** be written?

   A   vsrlohg
   B   urqkngf
   C   vsrlqhg
   D   urqkmgf

25. Which tile should replace the missing square?

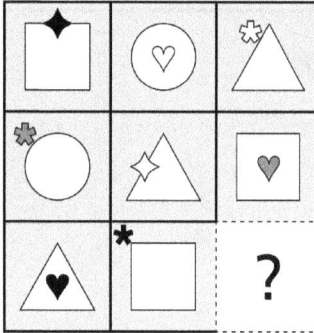 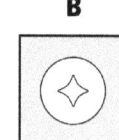 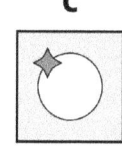 

26. Which phrases are closest in meaning?

   (1) a fool and his money are soon parted
   (2) to give someone a run for his money
   (3) to bring home the bacon
   (4) there's a sucker born every minute

   A   2 and 4
   B   1 and 3
   C   2 and 3
   D   1 and 4

27. A water tank when it is full of water weighs 36 kg. The same tank weighs 21 kg when it is half full. How much does the empty tank weigh?

   A   4 kg
   B   6 kg
   C   15 kg
   D   21 kg

28. In a class of 35 students, there are 4 girls for every 3 boys. What is the difference between the number of boys and the number of girls in the class?

   A   1
   B   4
   C   5
   D   12

29. Which is the odd one out?

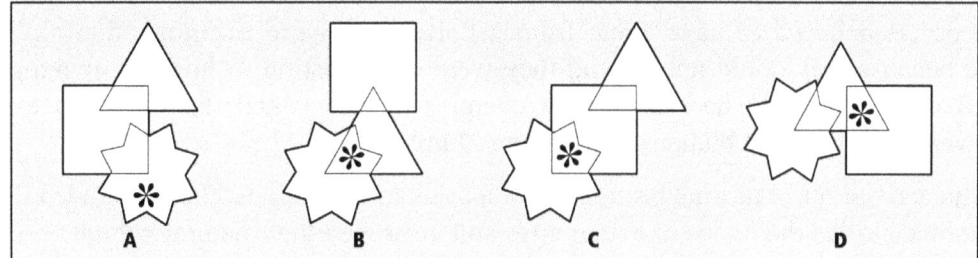

30. Choose the most suitable words to complete the sentence

   I asked John to (help / ask / give) me (lift / carry / pack) the heavy box (into / onto / around) the floor before I (packed / dropped / lifted) it.

   A   help   carry   around   lifted
   B   give   lift   onto   dropped
   C   ask   pack   into   packed
   D   help   lift   onto   dropped

Read the text and answer questions 31—35

The dodo bird

The dodo bird was thought by many people to be **imaginary**, like dragons and mermaids. But the dodo bird did exist once. Unfortunately, however, it has been extinct for over 300 years. The last recorded sighting of a dodo was in 1662.

Dodos were flightless birds. We know from skeleton remains that they were up to 3.3 feet (1.0 metres) tall. They weighed anywhere from 22 to 40 pounds (10 to 18 kg). Their closest relative is the Nicobar pigeon. No one knows what colour or shape their feathers were because only amateur sketches were made. There is also no information about breeding habits, behaviour or how long a dodo bird lived.

Dodo birds lived only in one area—the drier coastal regions of the island of Mauritius, which is in the Indian Ocean. They could not migrate to other islands because they could not fly. **This** is also the main reason why they built their nests on the ground.

Dodo birds ate seeds, nuts, bulbs, roots and fruit that had fallen from trees that they could not reach. They also ate shellfish and crabs. They even swallowed stones to help digest their food.

The name 'dodo' is believed to have come from a Portuguese word meaning 'dumb'. They probably earned this name because they could not fly and they were very trusting of humans, making them easy to catch and kill. Because the dodo had no natural enemies on the island, they had no experience with predators. They were curious about humans, rather than 'dumb'.

The sailors who arrived on Mauritius brought new species to the island. These included dogs, pigs, cats and rats. These animals killed the dodos, ate their eggs and destroyed their natural habitat.

You may have heard of the saying 'As dead as a dodo'. This saying is used when all traces of something that was once alive have been completely wiped out. The dodo is an important reminder that we must take care of all living animals so that they don't become extinct.

© MR STEGGELS ADVANCED INSTRUCTION PTY LTD

31. The author

    A   does not express an opinion about dodo birds
    B   suggests that all traces of the dodo bird were completely wiped out
    C   thinks that dodo birds should have been more suspicious of humans
    D   believes that it is important to conserve animals

32. The word **This** in paragraph 3 refers to the

    A   dodo bird's nest
    B   reason why dodos could not fly
    C   fact that dodos could not fly
    D   reason why the dodo bird could not travel very far

33. Choose the most suitable word to replace **imaginary**

    A   factual
    B   mythical
    C   magical
    D   spiritual

34. The dodo bird

    A   was completely vegetarian
    B   only ate fish
    C   ate both vegetables and fish
    D   ate stones because this helped them to feel full

35. We can conclude that the dodo bird probably could not fly because it

    A   did not need to
    B   had enough food on the island
    C   had no predators
    D   all of the above

END OF TEST

TEST 4

1. The letters in the word **meteor** can be rearranged to make a word meaning

    A   to learn off by heart
    B   100 centimetres
    C   earthquake
    D   distant

2. Rearrange the words below to make the best sentence

    students   books   read   difficult   some   tried   the   to

    What is the last word in the sentence?

    A   read
    B   difficult
    C   some
    D   books

3. The sums of the rows and columns are given. Only the digits 1–5 have been used. Each letter represents a digit. If the letter D = 2, what do the other letters stand for?

D	E	C	8
B	A	C	12
C	A	D	11
10	9	12	

    A   A = 3, B = 4, C = 5, E = 1
    B   A = 4, B = 1, C = 3, E = 5
    C   A = 4, B = 3, C = 5, E = 1
    D   A = 5, B = 4, C = 5, E = 1

4. In a packet 12 jelly snakes, there are 2 red, 1 blue, 3 yellow, 4 orange and 2 green. Which colour has a 1 in 3 chance of being picked out of the packet first?

    A   red
    B   yellow
    C   orange
    D   green

© MR STEGGELS ADVANCED INSTRUCTION PTY LTD

5. The numbers in each of the patterns below follow the same rule. What number should replace the question mark?

| 12 | 36 | 29 | | 9 | 27 | 20 | | 7 | 21 | ? |

- A 28
- B 14
- C 13
- D 11

6. Sally is shorter than Ronald who is taller than Rhonda. Rhonda is the same height as Susan who is taller than Sally. Which statement must be true?

- A Rhonda is the shortest
- B Susan is taller than Ronald
- C Sally is not the shortest
- D none of the above

7. What is the smallest 3-digit number that can be divided by 6?

- A 108
- B 106
- C 102
- D 100

8. Which number is missing?

$$34 \times \square = 136 \times 2$$

- A 4
- B 7
- C 6
- D 8

9. The word **ruffle** is most nearly the opposite in meaning to

- A flatten
- B smooth
- C calm
- D all of the above

Read the text and answer questions 10—14

Little Rid Rotten Head

Once upon a time, there lived a girl called Little Rid Rotten Head. An unusual name, yes—but she was no ordinary little girl. And this is no ordinary story.

One day, Little Rid's mother ordered her to take some freshly baked cockroach pie to her grandmother who lived in a run-down caravan park on the outskirts of town.

'But Mother,' said Rid, 'isn't it dangerous for a sweet girl like me to ride the subway on my own? After all, Rumble City has the highest crime rate in the country.'

'*Sweet little girl*? Ha!' cried Rid's mother. 'I baked that cockroach pie and you'll deliver it in person, or else. I haven't heard anything from that annoying old woman in months. Maybe she's sick. Or dead.'

'If she isn't, she will be after eating your stinky pie,' said Little Rid.

'What was that, young lady?' her mother snapped.

'I was just clearing my throat,' said Rid innocently. 'I'm sure Grandmamma will love it when I turn up on her doorstep with *this*...'

'Don't bet on it,' Rid's mother grunted and slammed the door in her face.

Rid smoothed out her dirty dress, fixed her tattered little bonnet, and off she went.

She hadn't even made it to the subway entrance when a large man approached her. He dug his fingers into her shoulder and pulled her face close to his. His teeth were sharp and his whiskers were wild and matted with dirt. 'Watcha' got in that bag, little girly?' he sneered

'Something that stinks worse than your breath,' Little Rid responded, holding her nose.

'Why, I oughta' string you up by your pigtails!' growled the man angrily.

'I'm not lying.' Rid raised the cockroach pie up to his face. 'Here; have a whiff.'

The big man took a deep breath in through his very large, hairy nostrils and instantly turned green.

I warned you,' said Little Rid, smugly. 'My mother is not only a bad parent but a dreadful cook as well.'

His eyes rolled back in his head. He swayed and fell onto the pavement, landing with a thump.

Little Rid quickly rifled through his pockets, removing his wallet and $300 cash and mobile phone, as well as his watch. Then she hailed a taxi and rode the rest of the way to her grandmother's house, safe from the terrors of the night.

© MR STEGGELS ADVANCED INSTRUCTION PTY LTD

10. What caused the man to sway and crash onto the pavement?

   A   Little Rid hit him with the cockroach pie
   B   The horrible smell of the pie knocked him out
   C   He turned green
   D   It doesn't say in the text

11. The man in the story is similar to a wolf in that he has

   A   very large nostrils
   B   sharp teeth
   C   wild whiskers matted with dirt
   D   all of the above

12. What is it about Little Rid Rotten Head that makes her no ordinary little girl?

   A   Her mother sends her to do dangerous tasks
   B   She knows how to use the subway and catch a taxi
   C   She enjoys eating stinky pies
   D   She is not a sweet little girl but a criminal herself

13. Which word means **attracted attention by whistling**?

   A   shoved
   B   hailed
   C   rifled
   D   cried

14. Following the introduction, the author

   A   recounts important events in detail
   B   outlines the features of the main characters
   C   adds more detail to the setting and characters by using quoted speech
   D   presents the strongest argument

© MR STEGGELS ADVANCED INSTRUCTION PTY LTD

15. Which tile completes the pattern?

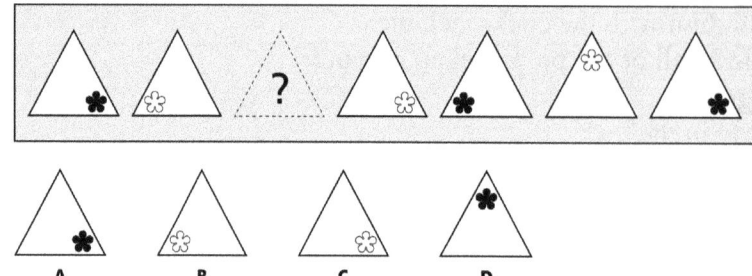

16. I bought a drink for $4.95 and a sandwich for $8.30. I paid with a $10 note and a $5 note. How much change should I have received?

   A $1.45
   B $1.75
   C $2.75
   D $1.85

17. What should you do with a **brochure**?

   A   eat it
   B   read it
   C   wear it
   D   hang it

18. Which letters are missing?

   Z A C   X B F   ? ? ?   T D L   R E O

   A   UCH
   B   VCI
   C   XCJ
   D   YCK

19. Which word is the most opposite in meaning to **vibrant**?

   A   vivid
   B   dull
   C   soft
   D   vital

This graph is for questions 20—21

FOOD ITEM	NUMBER OF CHILDREN	KEY
Sandwich	👤 👤 👤	👤 = 3 children
Garlic bread	👤 👤 👤 👤 👤 👤	
Pasta bake	👤 👤 👤 👤	
Spaghetti	👤 👤 👤	
Fruit salad	👤 👤	
Greek salad	👤	
Pie	👤 👤 👤 👤 👤 👤 👤	

20. The total number of children who ordered food items is

    A   26
    B   78
    C   81
    D   88

21. If 20 serves of spaghetti were prepared for lunches, how many were left over?

    A   17
    B   11
    C   9
    D   12

22. The bushwalking track is 120km in length. Starting at the 2km mark, there are signs every 3km. At what point on the track will the last sign be seen?

    A   113km
    B   118km
    C   119km
    D   120km

23. Two of these 3-letter groups can be joined to form a new word meaning **to grasp tightly**

   gra   mps   ats   tch   sti   spl   clu

   This new word begins with

   A   s
   B   g
   C   c
   D   a

24. What is the rule for the next shape in this pattern?

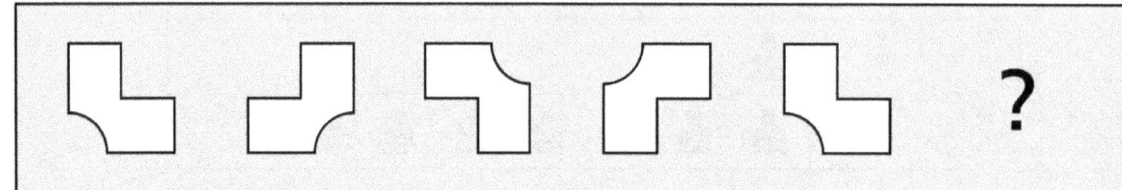

   A   Turn the shape 90° clockwise
   B   Turn the shape 180° clockwise
   C   Turn the shape 180° anti-clockwise
   D   Turn the shape 90° anti-clockwise

25. Three friends shared 39 marbles. Kate got three times as many as Aaron who got three times as many as Ray. How many marbles did Aaron get?

   A   3
   B   9
   C   12
   D   13

26. If the code for **ten** is **3w8** and the code for **lap** is **s6c**, what will the code be for **petal**?

   A   cw86s
   B   cw368
   C   cw36s
   D   cw36c

27. Unscramble these letters and choose which is **something you could not wear**

   A   letb
   B   edah
   C   ksco
   D   hose

28. Which is the odd one out?

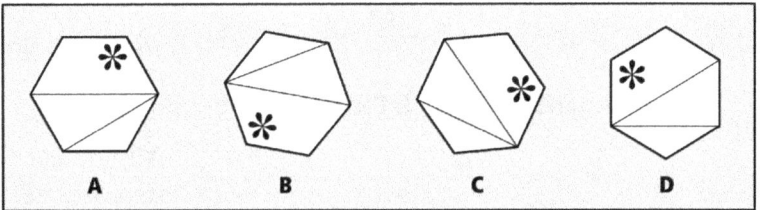

29. Which tile completes the pattern?

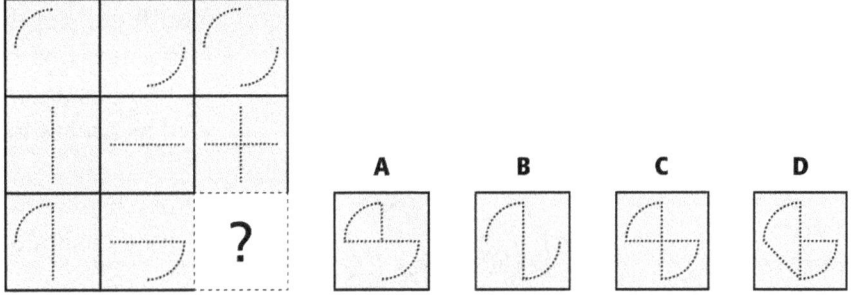

30. Which tile completes the pattern?

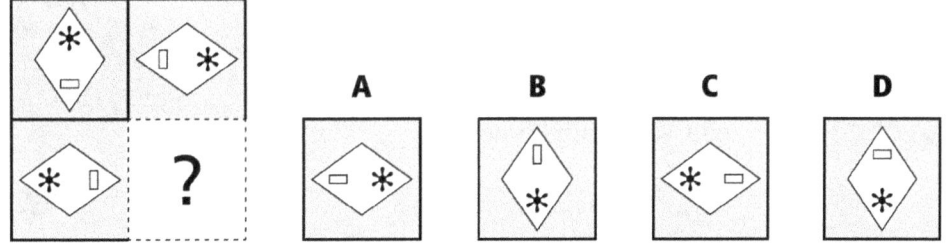

Read the text and answer questions 31—35

Turn your brains into cash!

Need extra pocket money but can't wait until your birthday?

Make your brains work for you from the comfort of your own bedroom!

It's so easy to get started. Just ask your parents for permission to join.

SIGN UP TODAY!
@
i.share-my-brains.com

Have you got a very good mark on an assignment or piece of school work?

Are you able to help other kids with their homework?
Do you have online access?

All you need is a PC, Mac, smartphone or tablet with Internet access.

Make great money!

Toys, lollies, games, music – work when you want and earn what you need during the busiest time of the day.

Your parents need to give access to a bank account so we can deposit your money!

Let our app lead the way!

You'll get step-by-step instructions on how to set up yourself as an online tutor, as well as access to 24/7 support.

Click UPLOAD and start earning cash today!

Kids need your help now!

The share my brains app lets you enter your details and be matched with kids doing the same work that you've already done.

Perfect for sharing your work and getting paid.

© MR STEGGELS ADVANCED INSTRUCTION PTY LTD

31. This text can best be described as

    A   an advertisement
    B   step-by-step instructions
    C   a report
    D   a poster

32. According to the author, the best reason to sign up to this app is to

    A   help other kids with their homework
    B   meet new friends online
    C   earn extra money
    D   work from the comfort of your own bedroom

33. A student who signs up for this app as a tutor must have

    A   access to the Internet
    B   parent permission
    C   a piggy bank to store their money
    D   both A and B

34. We can conclude that tutors don't need to prepare lessons or do extra study because they

    A   must be smart enough to help other kids in any subject
    B   are given step-by-step instructions and 24/7 support
    C   will be matched with kids doing the same work they have already done
    D   just tap and go

35. Tutors are paid

    A   in cash
    B   inside the app
    C   by deposit into a nominated account
    D   by the kids they help

END OF TEST

TEST 5

1. Which pattern comes next in the sequence?

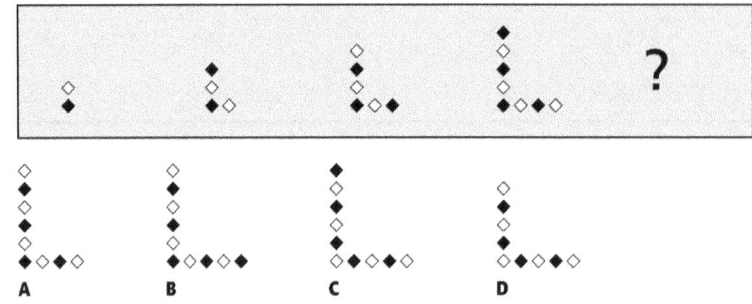

2. In a foreign language, **mita lit** means **did you** and **mita ewg** means **she did**. What is the foreign word for **you**?

   A mita
   B lit
   C ewg
   D you

3. My watch gains 3 minutes every hour. I set my watch to the correct time at 7am. What time will my watch show at 5pm?

   A 4.30pm
   B 4.27pm
   C 5.35pm
   D 5.30pm

4. The word **waste** is most nearly opposite in meaning to

   A recycle
   B reuse
   C conserve
   D rubbish

5. I can run 400m in 1 minute and 8 seconds. How long will it take me to run 100m at the same pace?

   A 17 seconds
   B 4 minutes and 32 seconds
   C 27 seconds
   D 16 seconds

6. A new letter can be added to the word **pride**. These six letters can then be rearranged to make a new word meaning

    A   tiring journey
    B   droplets of water
    C   an eight-legged animal
    D   fruit ready to eat

7. Which letter is missing from this series?

    A   d
    B   e
    C   f
    D   h

8. **Navy** is to **blue** as **lemon** is to

    A   yellow
    B   drink
    C   fruit
    D   happy

9. Which number completes the pattern?

    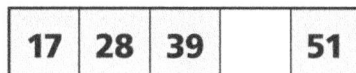

    A   50
    B   40
    C   41
    D   none of the above

10. Lemon drops are sold in packets of 3 for 20c. Mints cost 5c each. I bought 20 items and spent $1.30. How much of each item did I buy?

    A   6 packets of lemon drops and 18 mints
    B   3 packets of lemon drops and 17 mints
    C   2 packets of lemon drops and 18 mints
    D   5 packets of lemon drops and 15 mints

11. I bought a fast-growing bamboo plant that grew 0.5cm every day. At the store it was 1.15m tall. How tall was my bamboo plant 7 days after I bought it?

    A   1.185m
    B   1.45m
    C   1.50m
    D   4.65m

12. Solve this visual puzzle

13. I had a length of wire 24cm long. I bent it to make a rectangle. The length of the rectangle was double the width. What was the width of the rectangle I made?

    A   8cm
    B   6cm
    C   4cm
    D   3cm

14. These words all have something in common. Which word also belongs in this group?

        cherry   crimson   ruby   rose

    A   blueberry
    B   scarlet
    C   jam
    D   flower

15. **Germany** is to **country** as **German** is to

    A   French
    B   Europe
    C   language
    D   Germand

16. Which is the odd one out?

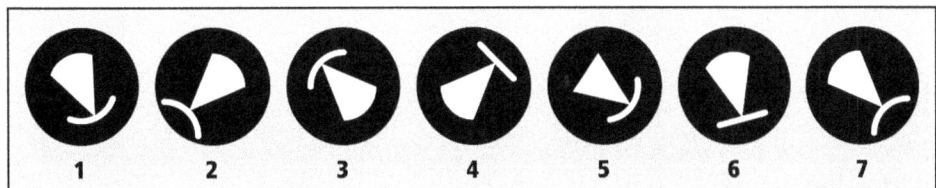

    A   2
    B   6
    C   7
    D   5

17. The square, triangle and circle stand for three different numbers: 3, 6 and 7. Which statement is correct?

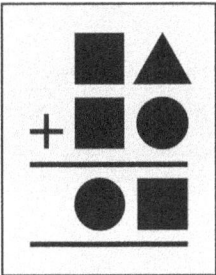

    A   triangle = 6
    B   triangle = 7
    C   square = 6
    D   circle = 3

18. Which phrases are closest in meaning?

    (1) to turn the tables
    (2) to foot the bill
    (3) take a short cut
    (4) now the shoe is on the other foot

    A   2 and 4
    B   1 and 3
    C   2 and 3
    D   1 and 4

© MR STEGGELS ADVANCED INSTRUCTION PTY LTD

Read the text and answer questions 19—23

Prepped and packed

Last minute gifts at low, low prices
New and exclusive
Small or large
Near and far
Two weeks only
As seen on TV

For little elves and big elves too
Picture book pack
Four books in each pack
Save $30 each
$69.99 limit 2 per customer

Cash back from Canon
Straight from Santa's workshop
Powershot Sandisk ultra 32gigabyte card
15% off 20% off 35% off *
Valid from 28 Nov to 15 Dec

Rescue dogs, top dogs, outback stations, drovers, salads, big shots, for beginners,
recipes, slow cook, family favourites, one pot, minute meals, bake, cook, natural, drones, dig and play,
mini-figure alarm clocks, desktop organiser, sim card starter pack!

So many choices
But only one destination
Show them you care
Show them **how much you care**
Have a little fun under the sun
Put a smile on their faces

*Excludes $20 gift cards

© MR STEGGELS ADVANCED INSTRUCTION PTY LTD

19. This text can best be described as

    A   an advertisement
    B   a report
    C   a poem
    D   a narrative

20. This text is mainly about

    A   the types of gifts people buy at Christmas time
    B   the way advertisers try to sell their products to customers
    C   showing the people you love how much you care by buying them gifts
    D   Christmas specials and deals at a store called Prepped and Packed

21. The first stanza

    A   creates a hurried rhythm by a repeating a pattern of word pairs
    B   introduces the topic of the text
    C   slows the reader so that they do not rush through the text
    D   lists the advantages of shopping at Prepped and Packed

22. The author used one long sentence in stanza 4 to

    A   increase the pace of reading
    B   show how many things are on sale at Prepped and Packed
    C   keep the rhythm of the text the same
    D   organise a list using commas

23. The phrase **how much you care** suggests that

    A   it is important to show others how much you care at Christmas.
    B   you should spend more to show people how much you care
    C   choosing the right gift for a loved one is most important.
    D   Prepped and Packed will help you to show others how much you care.

24. Which figure completes the pattern?

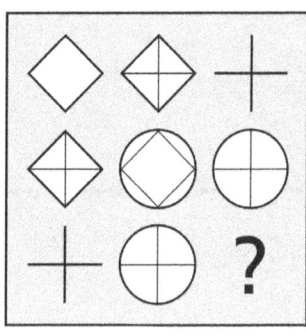
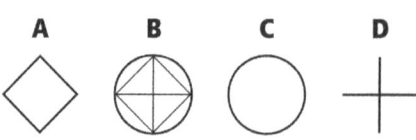

This graph is for questions 25—26

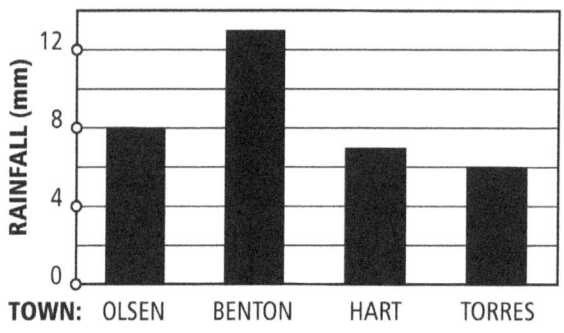

25. What is the total rainfall for all 4 towns?

    A   34mm
    B   35mm
    C   36mm
    D   44mm

26. What is the average rainfall for all four towns?

    A   exactly 6mm
    B   exactly 8mm
    C   exactly 8.5mm
    D   about 9mm

27. What is the name given to **a group of hounds**?

    A   a pack
    B   a posse
    C   a parliament
    D   a pod

28. Look at this clock. It is afternoon. How long is it until midnight?

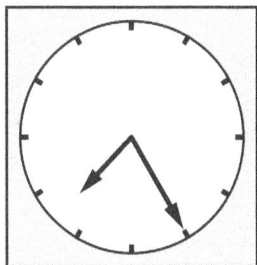

    A   5 hours and 35 minutes
    B   6 hours and 35 minutes
    C   4 hours and 35 minutes
    D   5 hours and 25 minutes

29. Which tile completes the pattern?

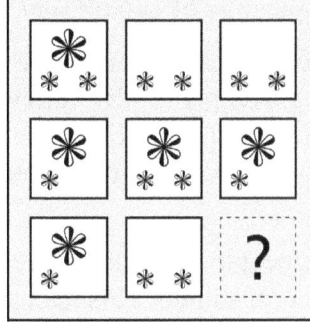 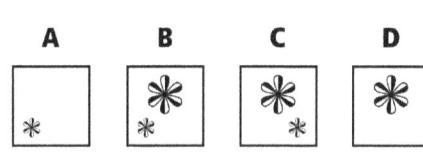

30. Two of the 3-letter groups below can be joined to form a new word

    tle   ket   ate   ust   loc   bas

This new word means

    A   find
    B   boil
    C   hurry
    D   carry

Read the text and answer questions 31—35

The Sahara desert

Countries	Algeria, Chad, Egypt, Libya, Mali, Mauritania, Morocoo, Niger, Sudan, Tunisia
Highest point	Emi Kouss, a shield volcano 11 204ft (3 415m)
Lowest point	Qattara minus 436ft (minus 133m)
Length	2 983mi (4800km)
Width	1 118mi (1 800km)
Area	3 552 140sq mi (9 200 000km squared)
East	Red Sea
West	Atlantic Ocean
North	Mediterranean
South	Niger River valley and Sudan region

The Sahara is the largest hot desert in the world. It is the third largest of all the deserts in the world after Antarctica and the Arctic. It is about the same size as the United States of America. It is one of the most severe climates on Earth. It has the world's highest average temperature of 116.6°F (47°C).

The Sahara is mainly rocky, barren flat areas. Contrary to popular belief, sand dunes are only a minor part, but many are more than 590ft (180m) high. There are also gravel plains, dry valleys, dry lakes and salt flats. The majority of streams and rivers in the Sahara are only seasonal. The Nile River is permanent. It crosses the Sahara and empties into the Mediterranean Sea. There are several underground aquifers. These sources of water sometimes reach the surface and form oases.

Thousands of years ago, the Sahara had enough water so that people and animals were able to live on its edges. A change occurred about 1600 BC when the axis of the Earth shifted. This lead to increased temperatures and decreased rainfall.

The screwhorn antelope is the largest indigenous animal in the Sahara. Rodents such as mice, rats, squirrels, snakes and scorpions thrive in the hot climate. Carnivores such as jackals, hyenas and foxes roam the desert in search of prey. Birds also live there, including the African silverbill and black-faced firefinch. Goats and camels are the most common domesticated animals in the Sahara. Camels can move quickly in sand and they can survive for 17 days without water.

Approximately 2 800 species of plants grow in the Sahara. These include acacia trees, palms, succulents, spiny shrubs and grasses. They have adapted to store water in thick stems to use in dry periods, and leaves or needles that help to prevent water loss.

© MR STEGGELS ADVANCED INSTRUCTION PTY LTD

31. The main purpose of this text is to

   A   record
   B   explain
   C   persuade
   D   inform

32. Which is true?

   A   The Sahara is the world's largest desert
   B   There are permanent oases in the Sahara desert
   C   The Sahara spans ten countries
   D   none of the above

33. The author has started the text with a table mainly

   A   to make finding facts and figures easier
   B   because that is the way most geography texts begin
   C   it just looks better than a whole page of paragraphs
   D   it is the most important and interesting information

34. We can conclude that

   A   underground water sources in the Sahara are what animals rely on to stay alive
   B   most people think that the Sahara desert is made up mainly of sand dunes
   C   no one lives in the Sahara desert anymore
   D   people/animals are still able to survive on the edges of the Sahara desert in large numbers

35. The Sahara became the third largest desert in the world

   A   because the Antarctic and Arctic are the first and second largest deserts
   B   due to people over-farming the land and using all of the water
   C   when there was a change in how the Earth rotated
   D   because of global warming and pollution

© MR STEGGELS ADVANCED INSTRUCTION PTY LTD

END OF TEST

Test 1 solutions

Q	A	Explanation
1	C	The word investigation is in the title of the activity
2	B	Now, use the Internet to research long jump record
3	C	There is only space for brief answers to questions 8 and 9
4	C	This time, when you jump, you are going to run.
5	D	World record (noun) Record those distances (verb) Long jump (noun) jump forward (verb)
6	D	Skip three letters AB cde FG hij KL mno PQ rst UV
7	B	2.5L + 1.9L = 4.4L 4.4 ÷ 2 = 2.2 (even amount) 2.5L − 0.3L = 2.2L 1.9L + 0.3L = 2.2L
8	A	lips = 8734 slip = 4873 silt = 4785 list = 8745
9	C	70 − (6 − 4) = 60 students on board to begin with. 40 + 20 = 60 (Half as many as boys as girls) 40 + 6 = 46 girls 20 + 4 = 24 boys
10	C	arid means having little or no rain; too dry or barren to support vegetation. A desert is dry.
11	B	1. The hashtag in the corner is made up of 5 lines, then 4, then 3, then 2, then 1 2. Hourglass, diamond alternates bottom left corner 3. The dot in the hexagon moves clockwise
12	D	Water is always part of river, estuary and stream, but not a valley.
13	B	66 ÷ 3 = 22 which is the middle number 21 + 22 + 23 = 66
14	A	1 square = two circles = 8 triangles
15	D	lifeguard lifeboat lifeblood lifeline
16	B	Att: is the abbreviation for Attention
17	C	angry: What are you going to do about it? official: Att: Mr Scott Sincerely, Mrs Heather Edwards
18	D	How are you? Tried to call but couldn't get a hold of you.
19	D	All the girls from our class were there, and a couple of the boys, too. I really missed you at my party. She made our favourite banana cheesecake too.
20	C	Clearly your teaching staff is not policing the school's No Hat No Play rule, which is clearly unacceptable.
21	D	souvlaki: a popular Greek fast food of small pieces of meat on a skewer massuer: a person who provides massage (French) bouquet: a bunch of flowers beret: a round, flat cap of felt or cloth (French)
22	C	Top number in table x 2 − 1 = bottom number
23	A	2 F 1R, 2F 1R, 2F 1R, 2F R1, 2F: a total of 10F and 4R

24	D	Doctors do not always work at hospitals, during the day or alone, but they always treat patients
25	C	HHH, HHT, HTH, TTT TTT, TTH, THT, HHH
26	B	Merry and glad are synonyms (similar meanings). Blunt is the same as unsharpened.
27	B	Answer C = flipped Answer B = then turned to the right 90° (¼ turn)
28	A	Butterflies fly and feed during the day.
29	A	1: W xy Z ab C de F 2: V wx Y za B cd E 3: X yz A bc D ef G
30	C	Derek: Area = 18 sq m P = 22m Leonard: Area = 12sq m P = 24m 12sq m x 1 ½ = 12 + 6 = 18sq m
31	C	A = plum B = orange C = spinach D = lemon
32	C	Shapes must appear in black, grey and white. The triangle appears in black and grey, not white.
33	C	Profit = $65 (money collected) - $25 (cost of making) = $40 40c x 100 = 4 000c or $40
34	B	From left to right add one square rotated clockwise 22.5° (22.5° + 22.5° + 22.5° + 22.5° = 90°)
35	C	Reverse alphabet code: | A	B	C	D	E	F	G	H	I	J	K	L	M	N	O	P	Q	R	S	T	U	V	W	X	Y	Z
---	---	---	---	---	---	---	---	---	---	---	---	---	---	---	---	---	---	---	---	---	---	---	---	---	---
z	y	x	w	v	u	t	s	r	q	p	o	n	m	l	k	j	i	h	g	f	e	d	c	b	a	

Test One score summary																
General ability	Question	6	8	10	11	12	15	21	24	26	28	29	31	32	34	35	Total
	tick/cross																
Reading	Question	1	2	3	4	5	16	17	18	19	20	Total					
	tick/cross																
Mathematics	Question	7	9	13	14	22	23	25	27	30	33	Total					
	tick/cross																

Test 2 solutions

Q	A	Explanation
1	B	Greg is reckless: he ignores the dangers involved in running into the tunnel Frank is cautious: 'I really don't think we should be here,' said Frank. 'It's almost midnight.'
2	D	Frank is annoyed and frustrated that Greg won't listen to him
3	A	Similes compare one thing with another of a different kind. They use like or as. The coaster train is like an angry serpent.
4	C	thundered: made a noise like thunder appeared: became visible loomed: appeared in a threatening way burst: a sudden, violent outbreak
5	D	Frank hears voices of children screaming on the coaster but the train is unoccupied, meaning that they are ghosts of children who died in "the accident".

6	C	A dessert is sweet course usually eaten at the end of a meal.
7	A	A mountain is high. A valley is low.
8	B	e.g. Cheap toys are more or less (almost always) a waste of money.
9	B	Possible numbers: 41, 43, 45, 47 & 49 24, 34, 44 and 54 are even so cannot be included
10	D	Ollie is the youngest. Ramsey is older than Ollie. Clara is older than Ramsey. Bill is two years older than Clara.
11	B	prime numbers have only two factors: 5 and 19 Ccomposite numbers have more than two factors: 10 and 24
12	D	months with 30 days: April, June, September, November months with 31 days: January, March, May, July, August, October, December
13	C	The teacher saw that there was a student without a hat.
14	A	RRRR + D = EEE RR = D so DDD = EEE so D = E
15	D	opinion means the same as viewpoint, outlook and judgement
16	C	238 x 2 = 476 68 x 7 = 476
17	B	a match starts a fire a key starts a car
18	D	1st floor: 2 2nd floor: 4 3rd floor: 6 4th floor: 8 5th floor: 10 6th floor: 12 8 + 10 + 12 = 30
19	B	Campsite to Blue Falls to Rocky Point = 2.9km + 13.8km = 16.7km 16.7 x 2 = 33.4km
20	D	C = vertical dashed line X = squares on each end of horizontal lines
21	B	Reverse alphabet code: | A	B	C	D	E	F	G	H	I	J	K	L	M	N	O	P	Q	R	S	T	U	V	W	X	Y	Z
---	---	---	---	---	---	---	---	---	---	---	---	---	---	---	---	---	---	---	---	---	---	---	---	---	---
z	y	x	w	v	u	t	s	r	q	p	o	n	m	l	k	j	i	h	g	f	e	d	c	b	a	
22	A	fullback: a player in a defensive position at the side or back of play backpay: wages and benefits owed to an employee for work already done
23	C	The shape is rotating 90° (¼ turn) anticlockwise
24	D	3 + 3 = 6 6 + 3 = 9 6 + 6 = 12 12 − 3 = 9 6 ÷ 3 = 2
25	D	1: black diamond is turning 90° (¼ turn) 2: trapezium flipping vertically
26	B	flammable: easily set on fire
27	C	These are all capital cities of the world. New York is a city, but not the capital of the USA. Mexico and Egypt are countries. Paris is the capital of France.
28	D	A = polo B = cricket C = netball D = court
29	D	Minny and Susan may be the same age. Both are younger that Tamara.
30	B	a wife has a husband a child has a parent (mother / father) a brother has a sibling a nephew has an aunt or uncle

31	D	persuade the reader to visit the website: Visit us today at www.hiphiphooray.com.au provide information: Our warehouses are stocked with a huge range of party essentials, including toys, games, and hand-selected gifts. attract new customers: Haven't shopped with us before?
32	D	exclamation marks: All cakes made fresh daily! italics: *made fresh daily* bold lettering: **All your party needs in one place!**
33	B	Rural or country areas are sometimes far away from cities and require long periods of transport.
34	D	New Year's Eve is an event.
35	C	coupon: a voucher entitling the holder to a discount off a particular product. discount: a deduction from the usual cost of something. expiry: the end of the period for which something is valid. voucher: a small printed piece of paper that entitles the holder to a discount, or that may be exchanged for goods or services.

Test Two score summary															
General ability	Question	6	7	8	13	15	17	20	21	22	23	25	26	27	28	30	Total
	tick/cross															
Reading	Question	1	2	3	4	5	31	32	33	34	35	Total
	tick/cross											
Mathematics	Question	9	10	11	12	14	16	18	19	24	29	Total
	tick/cross											

Test 3 solutions

Q	A	Explanation
1	C	length on both sides = 20 cm width on both sides = 15cm (20 x 2) + (15 x 2) = 40 + 30 = 70 cm
2	B	Broken and repaired are antonyms (words with opposite meanings), so are mean and kind.
3	C	jacket: an outer garment extending either to the waist, having sleeves and buttons brooch: an ornament fastened to clothing with a hinged pin and catch. tie: clothing worn with a collared shirt around the neck and knotted at the throat. beret: round, flat cap made of felt or cloth
4	D	c = @ a = ^ r = # e = > f = ? u = $ l = /
5	C	$5 + $2 = $7 $7.00 - ($2.85 + $1.75) = $2.40
6	C	celebrity: a famous person, especially in entertainment or sport. traitor: someone who betrays a friend or country unknown: not known or familiar unfamous is not a word
7	D	6.40 am → 3.40 pm is 9 hours 3.15 pm is 25 minutes less than 3.40 pm 9 hours less 25 minutes = 8 hours and 35 minutes.
8	D	250 has been shared out three times (total $225) which leaves $25 left from $250
9	C	error, blunder and slip-up all mean mistake. A lie is an untruth.

10	C	greedy = selfish
11	B	possessions = things that can be bought and sold. None of his possessions could fulfill him.
12	D	She gestured (showed him with her hands) further down the road (where she lived in the cottage beyond the brook)
13	B	What man does not want the finest of everything? This means: the finest things that money can buy.
14	A	a small clearing or area of grass where there were gravestones.
15	B	permanent: lasting or intended to last or remain unchanged indefinitely. solid: firm and stable in shape; not liquid or fluid. fleeting: lasting only a short while marker: a felt-tip pen with a broad tip. ancient: belonging to the very distant past and no longer in existence.
16	D	$32.87 + $12.95 + $3.56 + $2.48 + $0.96 = $52.82. Half of this is $26.41 which is closest to $26.00
17	B	Top number x 5 + 3 = bottom number 12 x 5 = 60 60 + 3 = 63
18	D	In A, B and C, the number of edges on the black shape equals number of flowers.
19	C	Group A: hand Group B: some = handsome
20	B	c = & a = # r = $ p = ! e = @ t = ^ s = %
21	C	myth: a traditional story involving supernatural events or beings have: to possess / own
22	D	$2.0 \div 5 = 0.4$ each division goes up by 0.4 so the 2nd division = 0.8
23	A	8 + 13 + 2 = 23 5 + 7 + 2 = 14 9 + 6 + 2 = 17 7 + 4 + 2 = 13
24	A	Pattern: skip 2 letters fwd. S tu V P qr S O pq R I jk L L mn O E fg H D ef G
25	C	1: large square, circle, triangle in white 2: small heart in centre (each in black, grey and white) 3: small diamond on perimeter (each in black, grey and white) 4: small asterisks outside shape (each in black, grey and white)
26	D	1: a foolish person spends money carelessly and will soon be penniless. 2: to closely challenge someone in a competition or contest 3: to earn a salary to bring home money earned at a job 4: there is no shortage of foolish people who can be tricked out of their money
27	B	Full water tank = 36kg. Half full of water = 21kg 36 – 21 = 15kg Half of the water = 15kg All of the water = 15 x 2 = 30kg Tank = 36kg – 30kg = 6kg
28	C	Girls: 4 Boys: 3 (7 students in total) Multiply both by 5 Girls: 20 Boys: 15 (35 students in total) Difference = 20 – 15 = 5
29	A	In B, C & D, the black flower is at the point of overlap between two larger white shapes. In A, it is not inside an overlap.
30	D	I asked John to help me lift the heavy box onto the floor before I dropped it.
31	D	The dodo is an important reminder that we must take care of all living animals so that they don't become extinct.
32	C	…they could not fly. This is also the main reason why they built their nests on the ground.

33	B	factual: concerned with what is actually the case. mythical: occurring in or characteristic of myths or folk tales. magical: relating to, using, or resembling magic. spiritual: relating to religion or religious belief.
34	C	Dodo birds ate seeds, nuts, bulbs, roots and fruit that had fallen from trees that they could not reach. They also ate shellfish and crabs.
35	D	The dodo bird had no predators on the island, and it had all the food it needed so there was no need for it to migrate.

Test Three score summary															
General ability	Question	2	3	4	6	9	15	18	19	20	21	24	25	26	29	30	Total
	tick/cross															
Reading	Question	10	11	12	13	14	31	32	33	34	35	Total
	tick/cross											
Mathematics	Question	1	5	7	8	16	17	22	23	27	28	Total
	tick/cross											

Test 4 solutions

Q	A	Explanation
1	D	The new word is remote which means distant or far away
2	D	The students tried to read some difficult books.
3	C	top row: 2 + 1 + 5 = 8 middle row: 3 + 4 + 5 = 12 bottom row: 5 + 4 + 2 = 11
4	C	red: 2 out of 12 = 1 out of 6 yellow: 3 out of 12 = 1 out of 4 orange: 4 out of 12 = 1 out of 3 green: 2 out of 12 = 1 out of 6
5	B	The pattern is x 3 – 7 12 x 3 = 36 then 36 – 7 = 29 9 x 3 = 27 then 27 – 7 = 20 7 x 3 = 21 then 21 – 7 = 14
6	D	A: Rhonda is the same height as Susan who is taller than Sally B: Susan is shorter than Ronald C: Sally is shorter than both Rhonda and Susan who are both shorter than Ronald
7	C	102 ÷ 17 = 6
8	D	136 x 2 = 272 34 x 8 = 272
9	D	ruffle: disorder or disarrange (e.g. someone's hair), typically by running one's hands through it. Also to upset someone (e.g. to ruffle someone's feathers)
10	B	The man fell immediately after Rid held the pie up to his face.
11	D	A wolf has large nostrils, sharp teeth and wild whiskers (facial hair) often matted with dirt.
12	D	Little Rid quickly rifled through the man's pockets, removing his wallet and mobile phone, as well as his watch.

13	B	shoved: pushed hailed: called a taxi rifled: searched quickly cried: yelled out
14	C	The conversation between Little Rid and her mother add information to the setting (Rumble City has the highest crime rate in the country) and character ('Sweet little girl? Ha!' cried Rid's mother.)
15	D	1: flower moves clockwise around the corners of the triangle 2: alternating black / white…
16	B	$10 – $8.30 = $1.70 $5 – $4.95 = 5c $1.70 + 5c = $1.75
17	B	Brochure: a small book or magazine containing pictures and information about a product or service.
18	B	1: Z y X w V u T s R 2: A B C D E 3: C de F gh I jk L mn O
19	B	vibrant: full of energy and life. vivid: intensely deep or bright, producing powerful feelings dull: lacking interest or excitement. soft: in a quiet or gentle way. vital: full of energy; lively, absolutely necessary; essential.
20	B	There are 26 figures altogether. Each stands for 3 children 26 x 3 = 78
21	B	9 children ordered spaghetti. 20 servings were made. 20 – 9 = 11
22	C	short method: 119 – 2km = 117km 117km ÷ 3 = 39 long method: 2,5,8,11,14,17,20,23,26,29…92, 95, 98,101,104,107,110,113,116,119
23	C	clu + tch = clutch = to grasp tightly
24	D	Turn the shape 90° to the left (anti-clockwise)
25	B	If Kate got 9 then Aaron got 3 and Ray got 1 multiply these numbers by 3 Kate gets 27, Aaron gets 9 and Ray gets 3 27 + 9 + 3 = 39
26	C	cw36s P = c E = w T= 3 A = 6 L = s
27	B	A = belt B = head C = sock D = shoe
28	D	A, B & C are rotations of the same shape D is the mirror reflection of A
29	C	The lines in column 1 are overlapped with those in column 2 to produce column 3 The lines in row 1 are overlapped with those in row 2 to produce row 3
30	D	Shape is rotating 90° clockwise from the top left
31	A	Text is advertising a company that has created the i.share-my-brains app
32	C	Turn your brains into cash! Make great money! Need extra pocket money but can't wait until your birthday? Earn what you need during the busiest time of the day.
33	D	Online app. Ask your parent for permission.
34	C	Enter your details and be matched with kids doing the same work that you've already done.
35	C	Your parent needs to give access to a bank account

Test score summary																
General ability	Question	1	2	3	9	15	17	18	19	23	24	26	27	28	29	30	Total
	tick/cross																
Reading	Question	10	11	12	13	14	31	32	33	34	35	Total					
	tick/cross																
Mathematics	Question	4	5	6	7	8	16	20	21	22	25	Total					
	tick/cross																

Test 5 solutions

Q	A	Explanation
1	B	1: Add one diamond to each end from left to right 2: Alternate diamonds black / white each time a new figure is made
2	B	mita = did lit = you ewg = she
3	D	7 am – 5 pm = 10 hours 10 x 3 minutes = 30 minutes late in total 5 pm + 30 minutes = 5:30 pm
4	C	waste / rubbish: rubbish to throw something away without using it recycle: convert (waste) into reusable material. reuse: to use again or more than once conserve: protect from harm or destruction.
5	A	1 minute 8 seconds = 68 seconds 68 sec = 400m divide both by 4 400 ÷ 4 = 100 and 68 ÷ 4 = 17
6	C	Add S to pride = spider = eight-legged animal
7	B	Skip 2, skip 3: B cd E fgh I jk L mno P qr S
8	A	navy is a shade of blue lemon is a shade of yellow
9	B	first digit: 1, 2, 3, 4, 5 second digit: 7, 8, 9, 0, 1
10	C	(2 x 20c) + (18 x 5c) = 40c + 90c = $1.30
11	A	7 x 0.5 cm = 3.5 cm = 0.035m 1.15m + 0.035m = 1.185m
12	B	Inside and outside shapes swap places
13	C	24 ÷ 3 = 8 the two lengths are 8 cm which leaves 8 cm for both widths = 4 cm each 8 + 8 + 4 + 4 = 32
14	B	These words are all shades of the colour red. So is scarlet.
15	C	Germany is country German is a language
16	D	figure 5 has a flat, rather than rounded top.

17	A	36 + 37 = 73
18	D	to turn the tables: reverse one's position relative to someone else, especially by turning a position of disadvantage into one of advantage. to foot the bill: to pay for something / someone especially when the cost is large take a short cut: choose a shorter distance to travel now the shoe is on the other foot: roles have been reversed
19	C	A poem is written in stanzas
20	B	These words seem to come straight from a catalogue of gifts for sale
21	A	New and exclusive Small or large Near and far
22	A	There is no full stop or breath in the stanza until the end. The reader is forced to rush in order to read them all in a single breath.
23	B	amount of money spent on gift = how much you care
24	C	any lines or shapes repeated in column 1 or 2 are not transferred to column 3 any lines or shapes repeated in row 1 or 2 are not transferred to row 3
25	A	Olsen = 8 mm Benton = 13 mm Hart = 7 mm Torres = 6 mm 13 + 8 + 7 + 6 = 34 mm
26	C	34 ÷ 4 = 8 r 2 or 8 ½ = 8.5
27	A	hounds are dogs and they live in packs in the wild
28	C	time is 7:25 pm 7.25pm → 12.25 am = 5 hours 25 minutes less than 5 hours = 4 hours and 35 minutes
29	A	only shapes that appear in both columns 1 and 2 appear in column 3 only shapes that appear in both rows 1 and 2 appear in row 3
30	A	loc + ate = locate
31	D	This is an information report on the Sahara desert.
32	C	Algeria, Chad, Egypt, Libya, Mali, Mauritania, Morocoo, Niger, Sudan, Tunisia
33	A	Facts and figures are easier to read in a table format rather than in long sentences.
34	B	Contrary to popular belief (what most people believe), sand dunes are only a minor part,
35	C	A change occurred about 1600 BC when the axis of the Earth shifted. This lead to increased temperatures and decreased rainfall.

Test Five score summary															
General ability	Question	1	2	4	6	7	8	12	14	15	16	18	24	27	29	30	Total
	✗ or ✓																
Reading	Question	19	20	21	22	23	31	32	33	34	35	Total
	✗ or ✓											
Mathematics	Question	3	5	9	10	11	13	17	25	26	28	Total
	✗ or ✓											